DATE DUE			

I am an
ANGLICAN

I am an
ANGLICAN

Margaret Killingray
and
Joanna Killingray

Photography: Chris Fairclough

Consultant: The Bishop of Tonbridge

FRANKLIN WATTS

LONDON/NEW YORK/SYDNEY/TORONTO

Joanna Killingray is ten years old. She and her family live in Kent. Her father, David, teaches at London University. Her mother, Margaret, looks after the home and does some writing and office work. Joanna has two grown-up sisters, Kate and Fiona, who work in London. She goes to the local county primary school.

Contents

Franklin Watts Inc
12a Golden Square
LONDON W1

Franklin Watts Inc
387 Park Avenue South
New York 10016

UK ISBN: 0 86313 427 0
US ISBN: 01–531–10388–9
Library of Congress Catalog
Card No: 87–50453

The Publishers would like to thank the Killingray Family and the Congregation of St Nicholas's Parish Church, Sevenoaks, Kent for their help in the preparation of this book.

Special thanks are due to Canon Kenneth Prior, The Reverend Jeremy Thomson, David and Wendy Crosland, Mike and Margaret Talbot.

Printed in Italy by Lito Terrazzi

The Anglican belief

My family are Christians. We are members of the Anglican Church.

Anglicans, like all Christians, believe in one God who sent his Son, Jesus Christ, to live on earth. They believe God sends His Holy Spirit to help them live lives that please Him. The Christian faith is divided into different Churches. The Anglican or Church of England, separated from the Roman Catholic Church over four hundred years ago.

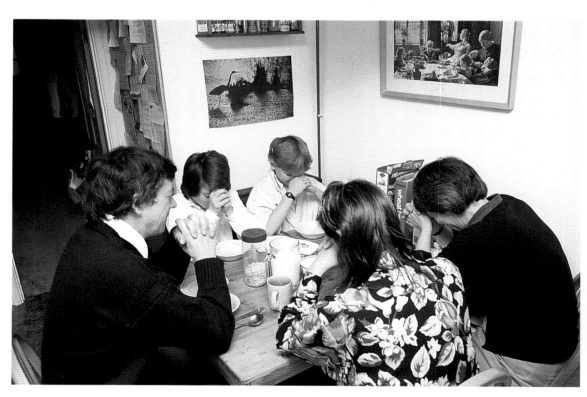

We have two Archbishops. They are the leaders of the Church of England.

The Archbishop of Canterbury (above left) is senior in rank to the Archbishop of York (above right). Under them are Bishops who look after an area called a diocese. Joanna's church is in the diocese of Rochester. The diocese has many parishes each with its own Church and ministers. The Anglican Church is the official Church for England. The Queen must be a member of the Church.

Going to Church

Our church is called St Nicholas. Around it are graves of people who died many years ago.

The parish church, named after a Christian Saint, is usually the most ancient building in any English community. In earlier times it would have been the only church. St Nicholas was built in the 12th Century. Today there are many types of Christian Church in most communities.

Once a month I go to a church
service with my family. We are
given song and service books at
the door. Bibles are always left on
the seats.

A Family Service is held on the first
Sunday of each month at 10.30 in the
morning. On other Sundays young
people go to a church school called
Junior Worship. There are services at
the church every Sunday in the
morning and evening. All services
last about one hour. Once people have
found a seat they usually say a short
prayer before the service begins.

The Family Service

The service begins with a prayer asking God to forgive us for our sins over the last week. Then there is a Bible reading.

The Ministers lead the service but other people, especially young people, do many things during the service. The Family Service is meant to bring young and old together in the worship of God. It is a joyful occasion for everyone. Here two sisters are reading a story from the Bible.

I am in the recorder group which sometimes plays at the Family Service. The Church Choir sings special hymns.

Music to accompany hymns is usually played on the organ. There is also a small orchestra of guitars, flutes and recorders. The choir is made up of people with very good voices. They have to rehearse at least once a week. The choir leads the whole Church in singing God's praises. Some hymns and songs come from the Anglican Hymn Book. In the Family Service many different songs are sung.

Everyone with a birthday during the next month is given a card. A Junior Worship choir then sings and there are more prayers.

The minister prays for those people with birthdays. He asks God to look after them all in the coming year. Anglicans use the Prayer Book for their services. In it are orders of service, including prayers that are used for confessing sins, the Creed in which all Christians state their belief and The Lord's Prayer. All these are said out loud by the congregation.

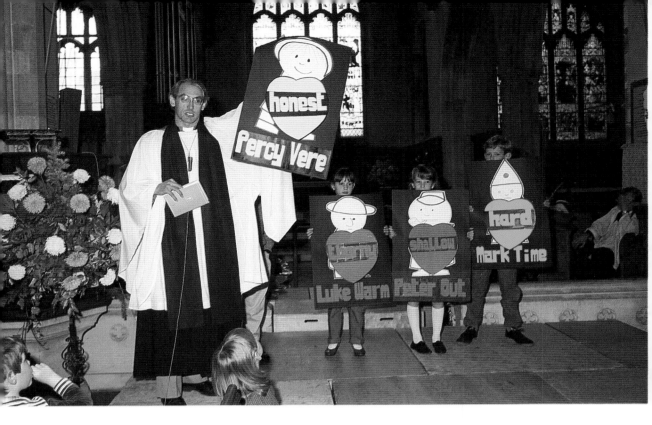

A minister always gives a talk called a sermon. He sometimes asks children to help him.

Sermons are meant to make people think about their lives and actions in relation to the teachings of Jesus. The speaker here is explaining the parable or story told by Jesus about a farmer seeding his field. Seed falls on different kinds of ground and grows well or badly. The same is true of how people respond to the Christian gospel. The service ends with a hymn and prayer. Many people then stay to talk and have a cup of coffee.

Baptism

Many babies are baptised at the Family Service. The Minister pours water on the head of the baby.

Baptism or Christening is the ceremony at which people first become members of the Church. The Minister makes the sign of the Cross on the baby's forehead. The parents and godparents promise to help the baby grow up as a Christian.

Getting Married

I like weddings very much. Everyone dresses up in their best clothes and the church is full of flowers.

The bride and groom promise to love and look after each other for all their lives. These promises are made in front of their family and friends, in the sight of God. The couple then sign the church Marriage Register which is a record of all weddings in the church. Photographs are then taken outside the church and everybody goes to a party called a reception.

Junior Worship

I go to Junior Worship on most Sunday mornings while my parents go to church. I play in the recorder group.

The church year begins a month or so before Christmas with a time called Advent. During this time Christians look forward to celebrating Jesus' birth and remember that He promised to come again one day as Judge and King of all the earth. Christmas is a festival for which special food is prepared: mince pies, puddings and a Christmas cake.

We write plays and act in them for the other children. We always end with songs and prayers.

All the children then come together in the big hall. The leaders of Junior Worship think of many interesting and enjoyable ways for the children to worship. The children write their own prayers and choose which songs to sing. There are prayers for anyone who is ill. When they reach eleven years, children move on to another Sunday School called Centrepoint at which they stay until fifteen.

Helping other people

At Junior Worship we also pack up parcels of clothes to send to poor children in Africa.

Junior Worship has for many years kept in touch with Jacaranda Cottage, a home in Kenya for about thirty boys of up to sixteen years old. The home is looked after by a married couple who provide a caring Christian family life for the boys. Some of the boys are orphans or from poor families. St Nicholas church takes much interest in such work.

We have seen many photographs of Jacaranda Cottage and the boys. We collect money at Junior Worship to send to them.

The house parents at the Cottage send back photographs and regular letters giving news of the boys. Prayers are said at Junior Worship for special needs at the Cottage. Two members of St Nicholas have recently been to Kenya and visited Jacaranda Cottage. They gave a talk to Junior Worship about the daily life of the Cottage.

Advent and Christmas

Christmas is a very exciting time. I count the days to Christmas by opening a window a day on my advent calendar.

The church year begins a month or so before Christmas with a time called Advent. During this time Christians look forward to celebrating Jesus' birth and remember that He promised to come again one day as Judge and King of all the earth. Christmas is a festival for which special food is prepared, mince pies, puddings and a Christmas cake.

I was a shepherd in my school nativity play. We have a huge Christmas tree at our church.

Christmas is a time of celebration and great joy for all Christians. The church is brightly decorated and most churches have a tree. At midnight on Christmas Eve there is a candlelit service at many churches to welcome the birthday of Christ. On Christmas morning a special service is held before the traditional Christmas meal.

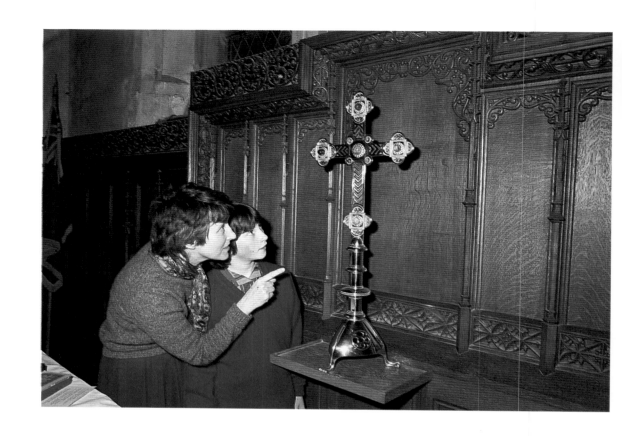

Lent and Easter

The Cross reminds us of the death of Jesus at Easter.

Lent is the forty days of preparation before Easter when many Christians pray more and give up some luxuries. At Easter Christians remember the last week of the life of Jesus on earth. He was put to death on the Cross, on what is now known as Good Friday. The Cross is seen as a symbol of God's love for man.

Easter Sunday is a happy day as Jesus came to life again. Pictures on the windows of our church show Him and His disciples.

On Easter Day Christians celebrate the resurrection of Christ from the dead. Christ gathered His disciples together and told them to preach the gospel throughout the world. The disciples started the Christian Church by telling everyone about Jesus and baptising those who believed in Him. The Anglican Prayer Book gives special prayers and readings for Easter as well as other festivals throughout the year.

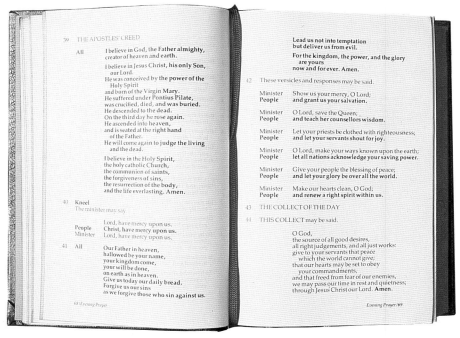

The church family

Sometimes we go away for a summer holiday together. We stay in a school and I sleep in a dormitory with my friends.

Members of the church see themselves as part of a large family. It is thought essential for everyone to get to know each other well. It is not enough just to attend a service on a Sunday. On each day of the holiday there is a talk on a Christian subject and a time for worship. There are also walks, sports and other outings.

We also get together on a day. summer. There are many things to do. We have picnic lunches.

In the morning people can take part in different hobbies, including knitting, drama, playing music, doing jigsaw puzzles and lots of other things. After lunch there are football matches and races. Days like this draw the members closer together, and those who are lonely can feel part of a family. After Family Service on summer Sundays everyone has a picnic lunch together.

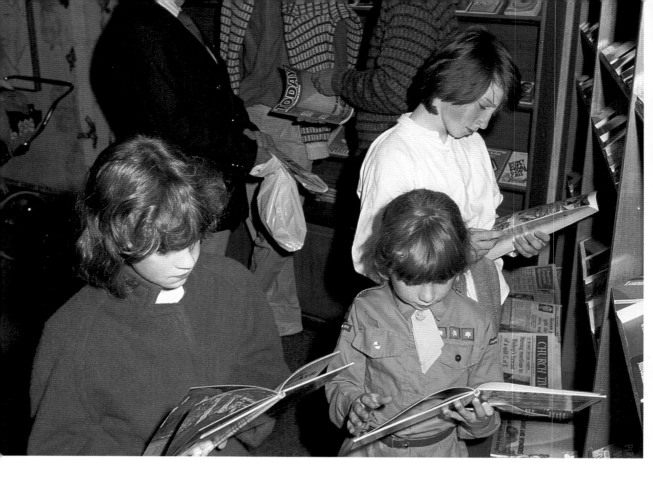

Learning More

At the back of our church there is a bookshop. Sometimes my friends and I look at the books.

The bookstall sells Bibles and a wide range of other books and magazines on Christian subjects. Bible study is seen as a very important means of understanding God. During the week small groups of church members meet to discuss the Bible and pray together.

Before I go to sleep I read the Bible and pray to God.

Joanna's family prays together, thanking God for his gifts and asking Him to look after them. Joanna will need to decide when she is older whether she wants to become a full adult member of the church. Once a year the Bishop comes to the church and gives a confirmation service when all those who wish to join the church make the promises that their parents and god-parents made at their baptism, for themselves. After being confirmed a person can take part in the Holy Communion service which recalls the last meal of Christ with his disciples. It is the most important service for all Christians.

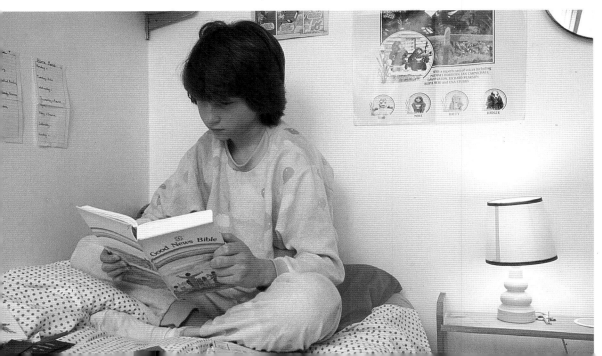

The Anglican Year

The church year is based on the normal calendar year but starts with the season of Advent at the end of November/ beginning of December. Apart from the major festivals some churches remember days named after saints.

CHRISTMAS DAY
25th December
The celebration of th
of Jesus Christ.

ADVENT
November/December
The season of preparation
for Christmas which begins
four Sundays before
Christmas.

NOVEMBER

DECEMBER

OCTOBER

SEPTEMBER

AUGUST

JULY

JANUARY
FEBRUARY
MARCH
APRIL
MAY
JUNE

PHANY
nuary
embers the visit of the
(kings or wise men) to
aby Jesus.

LENT
40 days
Begins on Ash Wednesday
and ends at Easter. It is a
time of prayer and fasting in
preparation for Easter.

HOLY WEEK
March/April
This begins with Passion or
Palm Sunday which
remembers Jesus' entry
into Jerusalem. Maundy
Thursday commemorates
the Last Supper at which
Jesus washed the feet of his
disciples. Good Friday was
the day when Jesus was
crucified.

EASTER SUNDAY
March/April
The day on which Jesus
rose from the dead. It is the
beginning of the season of
Easter which lasts for 50
days.

ASCENSION DAY
May
This is the Thursday 40
days after Easter Sunday
when Jesus finally left earth
and no longer appeared to
human view.

ECOST
Sunday)
une
st day of the Easter
when the Holy
came upon the
ers of Jesus Christ
ey went out to
t the gospel to the
world.

The dates of
Lent and
Easter change
each year
according to
the date of
Good Friday
which is the
Friday
following the
first full moon
after the
spring
equinox. Good
Friday is
usually in
April.

29

Facts and Figures

Christianity is the largest religion in the world, with about 1,000 million members throughout the world. About 700 million are Roman Catholics. The Anglican Communion, a worldwide fellowship of Churches derived from the Church of England, has about 47 million members. The Church of England has about 2 million of the 7 million members of Christian Churches in Britain. The Church in Wales, The Episcopal Church in Scotland and Church of Ireland all have links with the Church of England.

The Church of England is divided into two Provinces: Canterbury, having 30 dioceses (including the Diocese of Europe) and York with 14 dioceses.

The Archbishop of Canterbury is called the "Primate of all England" and the Archbishop of York is Known as the "Primate of England." A bishop is in charge of each diocese. The Parishes have a vicar or rector with assistants called curates. There were 13,400 Anglican ministers in the United Kingdom in 1985.

The Church of England's roots go back to the first Christians who came to Britain during Roman times. During the 16th century Christians all over Europe were challenging the authority and ideas of the Roman Catholic Church under the Pope. Queen Elizabeth I made the final break with Rome and established the Church of England as the State Church. The Sovereign must now be a member of the Church and uphold it.

The governing body of the Church of England is the General Synod in which the Archbishops, Bishops, Clergy and lay members are represented.

The Anglican Church bases its beliefs on the Bible which is divided into the Old and New Testaments. The Old Testament tells of God's creation of the world and the history of the Jews. The New Testament tells the story of Jesus Christ's life on earth and how the Christian Church began. The Anglican Prayer Book was written originally in the 16th century but has recently been revised into more modern English.

The Anglican Church is a leading member of the World Council of Churches which brings together some 300 different churches in over 100 countries.

Glossary

Baptism The sacrament in which a person becomes a member of the Church. Water is used to symbolize the gift of new life in Christ.

Bible The holy writings of Christianity said to be the word of God. They are divided into the Old and New Testaments.

Bishop A leading minister who is in charge of an area called a diocese which has many individual churches with their own ministers.

Communion The sacrament which recalls the last meal of Christ. Bread and wine are used to symbolize the body and blood of Christ.

Confirmation The service where a bishop places his hands on the head of a Christian who has decided to "confirm" the promises made on his or her behalf at baptism by parents and godparents.

Creed A statement of belief which is used by almost all Christian Churches

Gospel The word comes from an old word meaning "Good News." It is the name given to the essential message of Christianity. It is also used for the four versions of Christ's life in the New Testament.

Minister A person who has had training in theology and has been ordained by a bishop to lead the Church and to lead church services. At present only men can be ordained in the Church of England.

Parish Every part of England is divided into parishes each served by a church.

Prayer Book This sets down all the Church of England services and form of prayers for the year.

Resurrection The event when Jesus was raised from the dead.

Sacrament A ceremony with a visible sign of a gift to to a person from God. There are two, Baptism and Communion, which Jesus instructed Christians to do.

Sermon A talk given by a minister during a church service.

Sin The Christian word for wrong-doing and disobedience to God.

Index